Pip at the Pit

By Sally Cowan

Tam is at the pit.

Tam sits.

Is Pip at the pit?

Pip! Pip! Pip!

Pip **is** at the pit.

Tam pats Pip.

CHECKING FOR MEANING

1. Where was Tam? *(Literal)*

2. Who was Tam looking for? *(Literal)*

3. How does Tam feel at the end of the story? *(Inferential)*

EXTENDING VOCABULARY

at	Look at the word *at*. What word in the book contains the word *at*? What other words do you know that end in –*at*?
pit	Look at the word *pit*. What is a pit? Where might you find one? Can you think of any other words with the same meaning as *pit*?
pats	Look at the word *pats.* What is the base of this word? What has been added to the base? What is another word for *pats*?

MOVING BEYOND THE TEXT

1. Why do you think Pip was hiding from Tam?

2. Have you ever hidden from someone? Where did you hide?

3. What can you do in a sandpit? What tools might you use?

4. Where else can you find sand other than in a sandpit?

SPEED SOUNDS

Mm	Ss	Aa	Pp	Ii	Tt

PRACTICE WORDS

Tam

at

pit

Pip

sits

pats

sit

Sit